COWBIRD

Julie Marie Myatt

BROADWAY PLAY PUBLISHING INC
224 E 62nd St, NY, NY 10065
www.broadwayplaypub.com
info@broadwayplaypub.com

Cover photo by Julie Marie Myatt

First printing: September 2017
I S B N: 978-0-88145-435-2

Book design: Marie Donovan
Page make-up: Adobe InDesign
Typeface: Palatino
Printed and bound in the U S A

ACT ONE

Scene 1

(A dark, tacky bar. Night. The sounds of people laughing and talking. A young man sits at the bar; MICHAEL; handsome, but weary and worn for being only twenty years old.)

(MICHAEL lights a cigarette.)

CUSTOMERS: *(O S)* Hey Lorna!

(Lights up on LORNA COTES. She's mid-forties, well-dressed, attractive. She struts in waving to her friends.)

CUSTOMER: *(O S)* Where've you been, girl!

WOMAN: *(O S)* Where'd you go for so long?

MAN: *(O S)* Who'd you meet?

WOMAN: *(O S)* What'd you buy? What'd you bring me? Were you alone?

MAN: *(O S)* Who was he?

LORNA: You know I never kiss and tell…. Who wants to buy me a drink? All these questions are making me thirsty. You folks make talking to my mother seem like decent conversation. *(A drink sits in front of her.)* Now *there's* a welcome wagon. *(She drinks it down. Moans with pleasure. Holds up the empty glass.)* Who's next? Huh? Did you really miss me? *(She sees another drink on the bar.)* Now we're talking. *(She taps* MICHAEL's *drink in thanks, and takes a sip.)* To you, handsome.

*(*MICHAEL *smiles quickly, and shyly averts his eyes back to his beer.)*

LORNA: What's your name, kid?

MICHAEL: Uh…Michael.

LORNA: You look like an uh Michael.

MICHAEL: I do—

(A huge man pushes between LORNA *and* MICHAEL. BERT. *He picks her up off her bar stool.)*

BERT: There she is!

LORNA: I thought you were still on the road.

BERT: No, that was you! Feels like you've been eating well out there, huh?

LORNA: I may have splurged. Once. Occasionally.

BERT: You look great. *(He admires her figure and tries to kiss her cheek.)*

*(*LORNA *coyly avoids* BERT.*)*

LORNA: Not tonight, darling.

BERT: Why not?

LORNA: Busy.

BERT: With who?

LORNA: Since when do I have to explain my time to people? Jesus. I would have got married for that.

BERT: Since you started filling out that dress. Wow. It's enough to make me—

LORNA: Sorry. No.

BERT: Guess what I bought while you were gone?

LORNA: A new car.

BERT: How'd you know?

LORNA: You buy one every time I leave.

BERT: I get lonesome.

LORNA: What is it?

BERT: Chrysler.

LORNA: Ooo. Convertible?

BERT: Nice night.

LORNA: Convertible?

BERT: Maybe.

LORNA: Bert...

(BERT *slowly exits, waving the keys, keeping his eyes on* LORNA.)

(LORNA *returns to her cocktail. Feels* MICHAEL *staring at her.*

LORNA: So uh Michael...you in college?

MICHAEL: Me?

LORNA: You said your name's Michael, isn't it?

MICHAEL: Yes.

LORNA: You in school?

MICHAEL: Why?

LORNA: Why not. Seems like a good idea.

MICHAEL: Why?

LORNA: People are impressed by it. All that learning. Mind expansion.

MICHAEL: I finished.

LORNA: Well. Doesn't that just cock your pistol.

MICHAEL: I graduated. A couple of years—

LORNA: So...what are you doing with yourself now?

MICHAEL: I'm just—

LORNA: Besides sitting around here…killing innocent young ladies like myself with your wild good looks.

MICHAEL: Nothing.

LORNA: Oh. Interesting. Now that takes a lot of time, doesn't it?

MICHAEL: What?

LORNA: Doing nothing.

MICHAEL: What do you do with yourself?

LORNA: Plenty.

MICHAEL: Like what?

LORNA: I'm not drunk enough. *(To the bar)* Anyone got another one for me? Who's party is this anyway? Am I not a sight for sore eyes? Some fellow in Cancun, just the other day, after he stood gazing across the room at me, came up to me and told me that I literally Hurt his eyes. He said that I was so bright, so goddamn luminous that he felt this shooting Pain from his eyes straight down to his heart when he looked my way…

*(*MICHAEL *watches as* LORNA *lights a cigarette.)*

LORNA: So I gave him a pair of sunglasses, a visor, and some sunscreen and told him to tell me more.

*(*LORNA *catches* MICHAEL's *eye. Offers him one)*

MICHAEL: Thanks.

LORNA: It'll kill you.

MICHAEL: So will boredom.

LORNA: Can't argue there. *(Another drink for her. To the customers/bar)* I can't help it, folks. I love you. *(She kisses the air. To the bar)* And someday I'll prove it to y'all. One by one. My bed. My body. No strings attached.

(MICHAEL *watches as* LORNA *sips her martini. Enjoying every minute)*

LORNA: *(To the bar)* O K…maybe a Sunday breakfast or two. And some genuine compliments on my fine technique…but that's it.

LORNA: looks around, takes in the room.

(MICHAEL *looks around, following* LORNA*'s eyes.)*

LORNA: Nothing's changed here, I see.

MICHAEL: What?

LORNA: I've been coming here for fifteen years and they've had the same goddamn things on the wall.

MICHAEL: What?

LORNA: Those, those mirror things. Fifteen years of staring at the same faded ostrich asses or whatever the hell those are.

MICHAEL: I think they're vultures.

LORNA: Huh.

MICHAEL: Some call them buzzards.

LORNA: Really?

MICHAEL: Maybe.

LORNA: You a bird specialist?

MICHAEL: No.

LORNA: You won't catch a woman with that bird shit.

MICHAEL: It's just book stuff—I read a lot…of books—

LORNA: Good old-fashioned flattery will get you much farther. *(She winks at him, touches his cheek.)* You want to give it a try?

MICHAEL: What?

LORNA: How do I look?

(MICHAEL *doesn't know what to say.* LORNA *laughs.)*

LORNA: I leave you speechless, huh?

(MICHAEL *pushes a laugh.*)

LORNA: Well, you wouldn't be the first, sweetheart.

MICHAEL: Uh—

(LORNA *stands.*)

LORNA: A convertible calls. *(She finishes her drink.)* Ahh…see…that is pleasure. Absolute pleasure. The old Pacific is gonna sing sweet lullabies for me now. Oh yes she will. Wind in my hair. Sea on my skin. "Hello salty girl. I'm back." *(She dabs her lipstick with her napkin.)*

LORNA: See you bird man. *(She exits.)*

(MICHAEL *watches* LORNA *go.*)

(MICHAEL *slyly picks up* LORNA's *napkin.*)

MICHAEL: Martini please? *(He presses the lipstick marks left on the napkin against his own lips.)*

Scene 2

(A loud knocking)

*(*LORNA's *apartment. Morning)*

(It's one of those Southern California apartment buildings built in the seventies, and the matching furniture hasn't been replaced since. There's a few fashion magazines around, a couple dead plants, and a full bar in the built in the corner with bar stools.)

(A Spanish radio plays in the distance. Birds chirp.)

(A couple of new nice department store shopping bags are strewn about with boxes of shoes and dresses hanging out.)

*(*LORNA *enters with a glass of water and a bottle of aspirin.)*

(The knocking continues until LORNA *opens the door. Her neighbor* MAGGIE *stands on the other side of the door with a pile of mail. She's in her late sixties.)*

MAGGIE: You're fat.

*(*LORNA *takes the aspirin.)*

MAGGIE: Must have been a good trip.

LORNA: Uh huh.

MAGGIE: Ever heard of calling the post office?

LORNA: What time is it?

*(*MAGGIE *enters.)*

MAGGIE: You need to water these plants.

LORNA: I thought you were going to do that—

MAGGIE: Running up and down these stairs is no picnic at my age.

LORNA: I'll buy new ones.

MAGGIE: Must be nice. *(She wanders over to the bags.)* I don't know where you put all this stuff.

LORNA: Thanks for keeping my mail, Maggie.

MAGGIE: Sure.

*(*LORNA *holds out her hands to accept it.)*

*(*MAGGIE *hands over the mail.)*

MAGGIE: You have any bread in the house?

LORNA: No.

MAGGIE: Looks like you've been eating something.

LORNA: It's temporary.

MAGGIE: Every time you take a trip, you get fat. Seems like too much trouble to me. I don't like to diet.

LORNA: I know—

MAGGIE: You can learn just as much on T V, you know. You ever watch some of those travel programs? They're pretty interesting. You feel like you're right there.

LORNA: I'd rather be right there.

MAGGIE: Getting fat.

LORNA: Isn't it your lunch time, Maggie?

MAGGIE: I don't know what I'm going to do without bread. My delivery's not til tomorrow.

LORNA: You'll make do.

MAGGIE: They bring my food last now. All my groceries sit wilting in that kid's truck while he smokes cigarettes and shoots the breeze with all the other customers. I've been giving them my business for twenty years.

LORNA: Why don't you go down there and talk to them? *(She lights a cigarette.)*

MAGGIE: I will.

LORNA: Uh huh.

MAGGIE: I guess I can eat crackers. I've got some saltines in the cabinet from last week.

(MAGGIE looks around the apartment.)

MAGGIE: Did you bring me any—

(LORNA thrust a pack of matches in MAGGIE's hand.)

(MAGGIE reads the matches.)

MAGGIE: Arizona?

LORNA: Uh huh.

MAGGIE: I thought you went to Mexico.

LORNA: I met a guy from Arizona.

MAGGIE: What was he like?

LORNA: I don't know. Tall. Tan. Rich.

MAGGIE: Does he own this hotel?

LORNA: And seven others.

MAGGIE: Was he anything like that guy from Las Vegas?

LORNA: Who?

MAGGIE: The one that owned all those casinos?

LORNA: No. Arizona was sweeter.

MAGGIE: Really?

LORNA: Much.

MAGGIE: I thought the casino guy sounded nice. He spent a lot on his matches. That's a good sign.

LORNA: I guess.

MAGGIE: Really. Those are still the best I got. Next to the Atlantic City ones you stole in Spain.

LORNA: Right—

MAGGIE: But then I liked that Chicago man you met in London that owned that football team...what was his name?

LORNA: Chicago...

MAGGIE: You said he was real friendly and sweet, and big. Broad shoulders. Bill somebody.

LORNA: Oh, Chicago. Well—

MAGGIE: Oh Christ. My show's coming on. And I haven't even made my lunch. I guess I'll be eating those damn crackers. Welcome home.

LORNA: Thanks.

MAGGIE: Don't be stomping around up here. Remember. I'm a light sleeper. (*She exits.*)

(LORNA *closes the door and throws the mail on the couch.*)

MAGGIE: *(O S)* A kid came by to see you.

LORNA: What?

MAGGIE: *(O S)* Some kid.

(LORNA quickly walks and opens the door.)

LORNA: Why? *(She shouts up the hall.)* Why?

MAGGIE: *(O S)* How the hell would I know?

LORNA: What?

MAGGIE: *(O S)* My show's coming on!

Scene 3

(The bar)

(LORNA sits with a drink in hand, telling one of her stories.)

LORNA: So I'm running across the ship, in heels, and I look behind me, and he's still chasing me, he's still running as fast as he can, and I'm running as fast as I can, but I was a high school track star you see so I've got the calf muscles to beat him, even in three inch spikes, and he's huffing and puffing over his gold chains and Rolex—

BERT: But I thought he was the Captain—

LORNA: He was—

BERT: Why's he wearing gold chains?

LORNA: What?

BERT: That doesn't sound very Captain like.

LORNA: Why?

BERT: When I was in the Navy, no Captain of any ship I knew would be caught dead in gold chains.

LORNA: This is a cruise ship.

BERT: He's still a man of dignity.

LORNA: Not with a fifth of bourbon in his belly.

BERT: Disgraceful.

LORNA: All I could see was this blur of white running behind me when I slipped and fell in the pool.

BERT: He shouldn't be captain.

(MICHAEL *enters.*)

LORNA: I fell in head first and was soaked to the skin when all he did was stand there looking at me.

(MICHAEL *sees* LORNA *at a table and takes a seat at the bar.*)

MICHAEL: Martini.

LORNA: Didn't even lift a finger to get me out. Luckily, there was a fellow from Texas near by, and those men love to come to the rescue in such events and he reached down and pulled me out with one big oil money arm. We spent the rest of the evening drying me off in his cabin.

BERT: You only say these things to make me jealous.

LORNA: You only listen to get jealous. Now, go get me another drink, sweetheart... Go. (*She waves him off to the bar, and sees* MICHAEL.)

LORNA: Michael! Come sit with us. Buy him a drink while you're at it, Bert.

BERT: Why?

LORNA: He's handsome and I want you to. Now go.

BERT: I'm handsome.

LORNA: Of course you are.

BERT: Women tell me that I'm good-looking, Lorna.

LORNA: You are.

(BERT *shuffles off, passing* MICHAEL *on his way to the bar.*)

BERT: She's mine, kid.

MICHAEL: O K.

BERT: I've been waiting five years.

MICHAEL: O K.

BERT: Remember that.

(MICHAEL *sits down at the table.*)

LORNA: "Just do it."

MICHAEL: What?

LORNA: Your shirt.

MICHAEL: Oh, yeah. Nike. My father got it on sale—

LORNA: That's what I always say. Just do it. For Christ's sake.

(BERT *returns to the table, struggling not to spill the two martinis.*)

LORNA: And just drink it. Thanks, Bert.

(BERT *quickly sits as close to* LORNA *as possible.*)

LORNA: Are you trying to smell me?

BERT: What?

LORNA: You're not trying to smell me again, are you?

BERT: No.

LORNA: Uh huh.

BERT: But you do smell nice. Milky—

LORNA: So, Michael, you live around here?

MICHAEL: No.

LORNA: You on vacation? Come here to explore the wonders of the California coast? Taste the sun? Surf the big ones? I know some guys up in Malibu that can show you—

MICHAEL: No.

LORNA: You just here to drink? *(She taps his glass.)* Well. Then. That'll work. Cheers.

MICHAEL: Oh. Thanks. You're my mother.

LORNA: What?

MICHAEL: You're my mother.

LORNA: Oh…you want me to take you home with me?

MICHAEL: No.

LORNA: You want me to tuck you in?

MICHAEL: No—

LORNA: I can tell you a bedtime story.

(MICHAEL stares.)

LORNA: Hey…hey…you ever read that Dr Seuss book? Where the little tiny bird goes around to all these crazy things—an elephant, a fire hydrant, a bull dozer, an elephant—and he asks every one of them, "Are you my mother?" That's a sweet book.

BERT: I think my nephew has that—

LORNA: It's a great book.

MICHAEL: It is.

LORNA: You should read that, kid.

MICHAEL: I don't need to read it.

LORNA: I didn't say you need to read it, sweetheart, I just said you should. You might enjoy it.

MICHAEL: I know who my mother is.

LORNA: Well, maybe you should be nice and go over there and give her a call. Let her know you're thinking of her. Bert, there's only one olive in here. You know I like two.

MICHAEL: I'm thinking of you…at the moment.

LORNA: Might as well be talking to a bulldozer, kid.
Bert, get me another olive.

(BERT *remains seated as he and the rest of the bar seems to be staring at* LORNA.)

LORNA: Hey hey…what is this folks, a side-show?
Jesus. Don't you assholes have something else to do
than stare at me all night? I mean, I know I am pretty
"luminous"…some would say, "captivating", others
have said, "irresistible", but please…really. *Resist* me.
Go have some fun. Fuck someone at the bar.

BERT: He's your son?

LORNA: Get out of here! And get me a drink while
you're at it.

(BERT *goes to the bar.*)

(MICHAEL *removes a folded piece of paper from his pocket.*)

MICHAEL: That's your name, isn't it?

LORNA: I don't have my glasses.

MICHAEL: Lorna Cotes.

LORNA: It's a common name.

MICHAEL: "Born January 5th, 1955. Pampa, Texas."

LORNA: It's a large city.

MICHAEL: "Gave birth to a boy on July 8th, 1974 in
Saint Peters Hospital in Columbus, Ohio."

LORNA: Ohio. Let me think… Nope. Never been there.

MICHAEL: "Lorna Cotes' current residence: 1813 Ocean
Ave, Apartment C, Santa Monica, California, 90405"

LORNA: Which one of you turkeys is giving out my
address?

MICHAEL: "Birth mother has not responded to search."

LORNA: What search?

MICHAEL: You have a computer?

LORNA: No. I'm more of a people person. *(She grabs her purse.)*

MICHAEL: You can learn a lot these days.

LORNA: Have you been snooping around my house?

MICHAEL: No.

LORNA: Liar.

MICHAEL: I'm the one with the truth right here—

LORNA: You haven't been coming around my building asking about me?

MICHAEL: No.

LORNA: Then what brings you in here, Columbo?

MICHAEL: I am my mother's son.

(LORNA gets close to MICHAEL's face. Touches his cheek)

LORNA: But not mine. Sweetheart. *(She laughs and smiles and shakes her head as she exits.)*

(MICHAEL follows.)

Scene 4

(A parking lot)

(MICHAEL catches up with LORNA.)

MICHAEL: You know, you're a lot prettier than I thought you'd be.

(LORNA stops.)

MICHAEL: I just didn't picture that face…or the hair. You're much more glamorous really.

(LORNA laughs. She begins to light a cigarette.)

LORNA: Look kid, I don't know what you're trying to pull.

MICHAEL: What?

LORNA: This is where I live, where I drink, where I walk, drive, buy my groceries. My place.

MICHAEL: I know that.

LORNA: Then what are you trying to pull?

MICHAEL: Nothing. I just came to meet you.

LORNA: In my bar?

MICHAEL: Beginners luck.

LORNA: Bullshit.

MICHAEL: It's true.

LORNA: Do I look like a mother?

MICHAEL: I guess not—

LORNA: Hell, we could have even had some fun together. You and me. But this whole mother thing is a real mood spoiler, you know. *(She drops the cigarette and leaves it there.)* And those are my friends in there.

MICHAEL: They're fun people.

LORNA: I think so.

MICHAEL: I didn't mean to—

LORNA: Coming in and announcing to a room full of strangers that I am your mother… *(She laughs.)* What makes a kid do something like that?

MICHAEL: Twenty-five years of wondering.

LORNA: Oh really?

MICHAEL: You know how long I've wondered what it would be like to look at your face? To see what color your eyes were? The shape of your mouth?

LORNA: Listen…if I were your "real" mother, and I'm not, I would think, and I'm just taking a wild stab at this here, sweetheart, I would think that the whole point of giving you away was that she didn't have to see you again.

MICHAEL: Right.

LORNA: Be reminded.

MICHAEL: Uh huh.

LORNA: You can't just do that to a person.

MICHAEL: Yeah.

LORNA: So, just get yourself back to wherever you came from and sit down with your mom and tell her you love her. O K?

MICHAEL: What?

LORNA: I'm sure she's a good woman who loves you very much.

MICHAEL: She's dead.

LORNA: What?

MICHAEL: My adoptive mother is dead. She died two years ago.

(LORNA *is silent.*)

MICHAEL: It's true. *(Silence)* I know. It's pathetic really.

(LORNA *exits.*)

(MICHAEL *watches her go.*)

MICHAEL: "How can I move thee? …Will no entreaties cause thee to turn a favorable eye upon thy creature, who implores thy goodness and compassion…" *(He stops.)* "Believe me, Frankenstein, I was benevolent; my soul glowed with love and humanity; but am I not alone, miserably alone?"

Scene 5

(LORNA's *apartment*)

(LORNA *paces; anxiously moving about the apartment.*)

(LORNA *finally begins to wind down. Lights a cigarette and then pours herself a drink. She takes a seat on the couch.*)

(LORNA *finishes the drink. A drop spills on her chest. She wipes the vodka away, feels her full breasts underneath.*)

(LORNA *moves her hand down and rubs her belly.*)

Scene 6

(LORNA's *apartment*)

(MAGGIE *enters through the open door.*)

MAGGIE: Could you take your shoes off in the house.

(LORNA *enters with a handful of new plants, some mail, and a six pack of Slim Fast.*)

MAGGIE: Could you take your shoes off?

LORNA: Why?

MAGGIE: I can't sleep.

LORNA: It's four in the afternoon.

MAGGIE: So?

LORNA: It's still light outside.

MAGGIE: Still.

LORNA: Still what?

MAGGIE: I know you're wearing them.

LORNA: It's my apartment, Maggie. I can wear my own goddamn shoes.

MAGGIE: I don't know why you need to put them on anyway. Any minute there will be some man coming over to take them off for you, won't there?

LORNA: That's my business, Maggie.

MAGGIE: Well, I don't want to listen to it.

LORNA: Then don't.

MAGGIE: A woman your age running around all the time. *(She touches the plants.)* These are pretty.

LORNA: Thank you. Now, if you don't mind, I've got bills to pay. *(She sits down on the couch.)*

MAGGIE: Some people might wonder how you pay those bills.

LORNA: Don't you have a show to watch?

MAGGIE: That's a fancy dress.

LORNA: Yes it is.

MAGGIE: Looks like you paid a good bit for it.

LORNA: I did.

MAGGIE: Must be nice.

(LORNA begins looking through the mail.)

LORNA: It is. Now, move along Maggie. I've got business to attend to.

MAGGIE: What kind of business?

LORNA: I don't ask you about your days and you don't ask me about mine. That's the deal. So mosey on down to your piles of clutter and let me attend to mine.

MAGGIE: You could ask me about my life.

LORNA: I could.

MAGGIE: I wouldn't mind.

LORNA: Well, that's interesting, but I won't.

MAGGIE: That kid asked me about my life and I liked it.

(LORNA *keeps looking through the bills.*)

MAGGIE: He was a nervous type, short, but nice.

LORNA: Uh huh.

MAGGIE: He had some questions about you too.

LORNA: Oh did he.

MAGGIE: I didn't have much to tell him of course. *(Silence)* Told him you've been living here about fifteen years and that you didn't talk to me much.

LORNA: That's right.

MAGGIE: He said he would come back another day. *(Silence)* I offered him a Pepsi but he said he had to go.

LORNA: Don't you have to go?

MAGGIE: I guess I could. *(She doesn't move.)* I keep looking for you on America's Most Wanted.

LORNA: Do you?

MAGGIE: I do.

LORNA: Well, I'll let you know if I make it on there. I know you'd hate to miss it. What night's it come on?

MAGGIE: Saturday.

LORNA: I'll keep you informed.

(MAGGIE *heads for the door.*)

MAGGIE: You get a reward for turning people in.

LORNA: You'll be the first to know.

MAGGIE: Fifty thousand dollars.

LORNA: It's yours.

(MAGGIE *exits/closes the door.* LORNA *puts the mail aside, lights a cigarette and slips off her shoes.*)

Scene 7

(LORNA's *apartment*)

(BERT *sits across the table watching* LORNA *as she sorts through her stack of bills and letters. She tears up the junk mail.*)

LORNA: Don't you have something to do?

BERT: No.

LORNA: You giving up working?

BERT: Uh huh.

LORNA: What? Jesus. Am I growing a chicken out my face? Stop staring at me.

BERT: That kid does kind of look like you.

LORNA: You think everyone looks like me.

BERT: I do not.

LORNA: Every time you see a movie, you tell me so and so looks like me.

BERT: Because they are pretty, not because they are related.

LORNA: Well, if you want to talk genealogy, you'll have to take your ass some place else. I'm busy.

BERT: It was his mouth or something. His teeth.

LORNA: You're gonna see some teeth on your arm in a minute.

BERT: The way they show when he talks.

LORNA: Hand me my check book.

BERT: And his cheeks. You have the same cheeks.

LORNA: I have my cheeks. And you are never going to lay one speck of your cheek next to them again if you don't shut up. Now hand me that goddamn check book...Bert...stop staring at me and hand me that check book.

(BERT *hands it over.*)

BERT: His hands look familiar too. Didn't they?

(LORNA *grabs his hand and bangs it on the table.*)

LORNA: He is not my son, Bert. You hear me? So you can either sit there with your trap shut, or you can leave. (*She lets him go.*) I don't want to listen to you.

(BERT *rubs his hand, as* LORNA *begins to write a check.*)

(BERT *watches her write, looks around the room, rubs his hand, looks at his hand.*)

BERT: I always wanted a son.

(LORNA *points to the door.*)

Scene 8

(*The bar*)

(MICHAEL *sits at the bar alone with a pitcher of beer.*)

(BERT *enters still rubbing the pain out of his hand.*)

BERT: A little slow this time of day.

MICHAEL: Yeah.

BERT: No bartender?

MICHAEL: He went to lunch.

BERT: Huh. (*Silence*) Your father must have been a foreigner.

MICHAEL: What?

BERT: Your father. I don't think he was American.

MICHAEL: Why?

BERT: Lorna doesn't really take to us. She's likes things imported.

MICHAEL: I don't know.

BERT: You don't know what.

MICHAEL: Where my father was from.

BERT: Huh.

MICHAEL: Do you?

BERT: What?

MICHAEL: Know anything—

BERT: I barely know where Lorna's from…. She doesn't like to talk much about those things.

MICHAEL: Really.

(MICHAEL *pours* BERT *a beer.*)

BERT: Where are you staying?

MICHAEL: In a motel.

BERT: Did you fly out here?

MICHAEL: Drove.

BERT: Where from?

MICHAEL: Pittsburg.

BERT: Nice town.

MICHAEL: Not really.

BERT: You drive all the way out here just to meet Lorna?

MICHAEL: Uh…yes. I guess you could say that.

BERT: That's a long way.

MICHAEL: It is.

BERT: Was it worth it?

MICHAEL: I don't know yet.

BERT: Hell…she'll warm up to you.

MICHAEL: You think so.

BERT: If she's your mother.

MICHAEL: She is.

BERT: She's bound to love you.

MICHAEL: I'm not looking for her love.

BERT: Of course you are.

MICHAEL: I'm not.

BERT: What do you want?

MICHAEL: Do I have to want something?

BERT: You drove across the country.

MICHAEL: I'm young. There's a lot to see.

BERT: Huh.

(MICHAEL *nods.*)

BERT: So why you hanging out here?

(LORNA *enters.*)

LORNA: I need a ride to the bank.

BERT: Sit down a minute.

LORNA: I don't drink this time of day.

BERT: Ha. Are you trying to impress your son?

LORNA: No—

BERT: Sit down—

LORNA: He's not my son.

(MICHAEL *fishes through his pockets.*)

MICHAEL: I have baby pictures.

BERT: Do you now? Let's see.

MICHAEL: Some are a little worn.

BERT: Lorna, come look.

LORNA: I'm not interested.

BERT: Everyone likes to look at babies. C'mon.

(LORNA *remains standing by the door.*)

BERT: Will you look at that...what a face. What a face.

MICHAEL: Yeah.

BERT: It's perfect.

MICHAEL: I, a, I did do a few local modeling jobs for baby food.

BERT: No kidding? I'd buy food from your face. I would.

MICHAEL: My parents were stopped on the street. Some guy owned an advertising agency and wanted to use me.

BERT: And look at that one...what were you, two or so?

MICHAEL: One and a half.

BERT: Lord.

MICHAEL: My mother made all my clothes.

BERT: That's some outfit.

MICHAEL: It was hell. Look at me.

BERT: I know.

MICHAEL: Might as well be holding a tin cup and dancing to an accordion.

BERT: The hat is a little small.

MICHAEL: I look ridiculous.

LORNA: Bert. Do you mind?

BERT: There's some cute stuff here, Lorna.

LORNA: I'm not interested in cute stuff. I need a ride.

BERT: Oh, look at that...is that a hamster you've got there?

MICHAEL: Robert McGee. He eventually ran himself to death on his wheel, but he was sweet. In his way.

BERT: I had a turtle.

MICHAEL: Really?

BERT: Never did come out of it's shell.

MICHAEL: They're like that.

BERT: I think my father got it on sale.

LORNA: Bert!

BERT: What?

LORNA: I have got plans.

(BERT *throws* LORNA *the keys.*)

BERT: Go do them.

LORNA: I thought you were taking me to lunch.

BERT: Right. Look at that new bike.

MICHAEL: I won it, actually—

LORNA: Bert?

BERT: Michael, have you eaten?

MICHAEL: Uh. No. Not yet.

Scene 9

(LORNA'*s apartment*)

(BERT, LORNA *and* MICHAEL *all look ill.*)

BERT: Now that was something.

LORNA: Ten bucks for a pile of backyard weeds.

MICHAEL: Thanks for lunch. Good organic restaurants are sometimes hard to—

BERT: Fastest meal I've ever had.

MICHAEL: I guess I was kind of hungry—

BERT: If you two aren't related, then peas don't belong in pods. Good Lord. That waiter didn't have time to clear his throat to take our order before he was putting down the check.

LORNA: I think there was dirt in my salad.

(MICHAEL *takes in the apartment.*)

MICHAEL: A lot of minerals in dirt. I hear some places in Texas people actually eat the local land—

LORNA: Bathroom's back there.

(MICHAEL *exits.*)

LORNA: He's out of here in five minutes, Bert, or you're never getting near my bed again, much less—

BERT: I like him.

LORNA: Well, good for you. I don't have time for new friends. I've got plenty.

BERT: He's your son.

LORNA: If I've said it once, I've said it fifteen fucking too many times, that kid is not my son.

(*A knock at the door*)

LORNA: I'd think I'd know if I had been anyone's mother. Don't you?

(*Another knock*)

(LORNA *opens the door.* BEN, *twenty-three, stands on the other side.*)

BEN: LORNA Cotes?

LORNA: I'm not buying. (*She tries to close the door.*)

BEN: I think you're my mother.

LORNA: Sorry?

BEN: My mother.

(MICHAEL *enters from the bathroom.*)

(BEN *sneaks through the door.*)

BEN: You're Lorna Cotes?

LORNA: Maybe.

BEN: Well…I was born June 20, 1976, in Louisville, Kentucky? I was adopted by Doctor Benjamin and Margaret Goldberg?

LORNA: And?

BEN: Six pounds six ounces?

LORNA: Is that supposed to mean something to me?

BEN: Well, you're my mother.

LORNA: I'm not.

BEN: I think you are.

LORNA: You're mistaken.

BEN: No…no I'm not…I got it all right here… *(He stares at her.)* Don't you remember?

LORNA: No.

BEN: Twelve hours of labor?

LORNA: And?

(BEN pulls up his shirt.)

BEN: I have a birth mark on my stomach?

LORNA: Please. *(She pulls down his shirt.)* I don't want to see your skin.

BEN: My head was covered in hair?

(LORNA walks away from him. BEN follows.)

BEN: My eyes were closed shut.

(LORNA won't look at BEN.)

BEN: My father must have been Asian or—

LORNA: I don't care. I'm not a D N A specialist.

BEN: I didn't think you were, ma'am.

LORNA: So why don't you take your hair and spotted stomach and this boy over here. *(She grabs* BEN *and pulls* MICHAEL *to the door.)* And get out of my house. I'm not interested in your birthmarks or your story.

MICHAEL: Do you have records with you?

BEN: Uh huh.

MICHAEL: Let me see them.

*(*BEN *hands the papers over to* MICHAEL. LORNA *tries to rip them from his hands but he holds on.)*

LORNA: This is not a fucking orphanage—

BERT: They know that—

LORNA: Obviously they don't, Bert, because I am being invaded here. You see that?! I'm not interested in any Oliver fucking Twist breathing down my neck! So take your papers and dates and ounces and pounds and your goddamn desperate eyes out of here—

MICHAEL: It's her alright. I've got the same— *(He pulls the paper from his back pocket.)*

LORNA: This is my house!

*(*LORNA *pushes them out the door. Slams and locks it behind them)*

BERT: Lorna. *(He stands staring.)*

LORNA: Don't look at me like that. *(She grabs the bottle of booze.)*

Scene 10

(The hall)

BEN: No father.

*(*BEN *and* MICHAEL *stand comparing papers.)*

MICHAEL: Same here. Nothing.

BEN: Did you ask her?

MICHAEL: I don't know if she knows.

BEN: Really?

MICHAEL: Does that surprise you?

BEN: Well, she slept with the guy. They had sex.

(MICHAEL *laughs.*)

BEN: What?

MICHAEL: I'm guessing she's slept with many.

BEN: Why? What's she like?

MICHAEL: Well...the best that I can tell, she's pretty friendly. Likes to drink. Kind of funny. Unless you tell her she's your mother.

BEN: Huh.

MICHAEL: Things kind of went down hill from there.

(Silence)

BEN: My mom gave me the plane ticket out here.

MICHAEL: Really?

BEN: For my birthday.

MICHAEL: Nice.

BEN: Yeah, but I've been out here for a month and this is the first chance I've had to meet her.

(MICHAEL *nods.*)

BEN: Half my summer is almost gone.

MICHAEL: I guess so.

(Silence)

BEN: My mom's afraid I'll never come back.

MICHAEL: No worry of that, huh?

(BEN *and* MICHAEL *stand staring at each other.*)

(MICHAEL *lights a cigarette. Offers one to* BEN)

BEN: No, thanks.

(MICHAEL *puts the cigarettes away.*)

(BEN *checks his watch. Silence*)

BEN: Do, do you have a birth mark?

MICHAEL: No.

BEN: I didn't think so.

(BEN *and* MICHAEL *stare at each other.*)

MICHAEL: Are you afraid of heights?

BEN: No—

MICHAEL: Well, I'm not afraid of all heights. Just the really tall ones.

BEN: I hate eggs.

(*Silence*)

MICHAEL: I like them.

BEN: Bacon?

MICHAEL: With the eggs.

BEN: Do you wear glasses?

MICHAEL: No. Do you?

BEN: Contacts.

MICHAEL: I'm an insomniac.

BEN: Really?

MICHAEL: Yeah.

BEN: That's too bad. I used to wet the bed.

MICHAEL: Really?

BEN: Not—not anymore.

MICHAEL: You like your parents?

BEN: What?

MICHAEL: Your parents. Are they nice?

BEN: Oh. Yeah. Sure. They're great.

MICHAEL: Yeah?

BEN: I love them.

MICHAEL: That's good.

BEN: You?

MICHAEL: You want a beer?

BEN: No.

MICHAEL: Do you drink?

BEN: Not, not often. Never really—

MICHAEL: Do you want to?

BEN: I don't think so.

MICHAEL: Well. Hell. What's a brother for?

Scene 11

(LORNA's apartment)

(BERT now sits at the table, but still looks away from LORNA.)

(LORNA sits on the couch with a bottle of vodka.)

LORNA: Whining at me and sniffing around like two fucking lost puppies.

BERT: They seem like good—

LORNA: I'm not talking to you.

BERT: Fine.

LORNA: I lead a quiet life, don't I? I mean, I don't go around looking for trouble or talking about myself or bragging about things, do?

BERT: Well, yes, sometimes—

LORNA: Shut up.

BERT: Occasionally.

LORNA: Since when can boys show up and grab on
to your fucking dress hem and scratch into your eyes
with their voices and tell you you are their mother?
Since when can they do that? Just walk in like some
kind of mailman and announce that they are delivering
themselves to you, like it or not, and you've got no say
in the matter?

BERT: Are they your kids?

LORNA: What's it matter?

BERT: It matters to them, Lorna—

LORNA: Why are you still here?

BERT: I thought you might want some company—

LORNA: What's it matter what I want? Huh? Seems it
doesn't matter, does it? It's all about them. What they
need. I am not responsible for them. I am not.

BERT: Why'd you have them?

LORNA: That's none of your business.

BERT: You had them, gave them away—

LORNA: To good families! To good families. To lonely
fucking couples! People foaming at the mouth for
babies! Those kids are lucky! And they come back here
looking me in the eye like I did something wrong!

BERT: That's not what they're doing—

LORNA: They want to know Why…they want me to sit
them down on my knee and rub their foreheads and
tell them I did what was best for all of us and then
they want me to touch their cheeks and tell them I love
them and that never a day has gone by that I haven't
thought of them…and then they want me to take
them into my arms and cry and tell them how much

I've missed them and how sorry I am, they want me
to smooth down their hair, tell them what fine men
they've become…but I won't do it! I won't.

BERT: Then don't.

LORNA: I won't. That's not what I'm here for. No sir.
That's not my part. I gave birth for Christ's sake—-I
may have given birth to those kids but that's it. They
are lucky! Don't they see that! One day in a doctor's
office and they could have been air. Scraped clean.
Could have been tossed into a bucket of red blood
clots. The end. They could have been nothings. But no.
No. That's not what happened. Sacrifices were made.
A body was stretched and pulled out of shape just to
house them. Screams of pain were shouted through
clinched, gnashed teeth just to bring them forth. But
they are here, aren't they? They are here. Because of
me.

BERT: You are responsi—

LORNA: You don't bother the stork once it's done. No
sir. You don't come asking for more. You don't come
till up the cabbage patch. They already got all they are
getting from me. That's it. Breath of life is all you get
from me, kids.

BERT: Fine.

LORNA: I'm not talking to you.

Scene 12

(*The beach*)

(BEN *and* MICHAEL *sit with beers in hand.* MICHAEL's *shirt
is off. He's got scars on his chest.*)

MICHAEL: Look at that…that bird only has one foot.

BEN: I wonder what happened to the other one.

MICHAEL: I don't know.

BEN: Maybe it was born that way. I think that happens sometimes.

MICHAEL: He doesn't seem to mind, does he.

BEN: No.

MICHAEL: A little one-legged Casanova. Horny bastard. He probably told her he was Jonathan Livingston.

BEN: Who's that?

MICHAEL: A famous seagull.

BEN: No...

MICHAEL: He's got his own book.

BEN: Really?

MICHAEL: He's a spiritual bird.

BEN: Huh.

MICHAEL: What about you?

BEN: What?

MICHAEL: Your parents raise you religious or anything?

BEN: We're Jewish.

MICHAEL: You like it?

BEN: I guess so.

MICHAEL: You guess so.

BEN: I don't know anything else.

MICHAEL: You like wearing that, that, that yarmulke?

BEN: You get used to it.

MICHAEL: I hear it's a good religion. If you're into that.

BEN: What?

MICHAEL: That.

BEN: You're not?

MICHAEL: No… It's like trying to catch a fucking fly in a box. You have to believe that if you caught it and it's in there…you just have to believe it's in there.

BEN: Why?

MICHAEL: Because if you don't believe it's in there… and you try and open the box to make sure, maybe it'll fly out. Gone. You gotta believe it's in there or you may lose it, right?

BEN: I don't know—

MICHAEL: No. Might as well leave the fly alone. And the box.

BEN: Your parents aren't religious.

MICHAEL: The closest my father ever got is when he said, "Goddamn it!" as his hand went across my face.

BEN: Huh.

MICHAEL: He wanted a quieter son.

BEN: And your Mom?

MICHAEL: She wanted a quieter life.

BEN: And you?

MICHAEL: What?

BEN: What do you want?

MICHAEL: We don't look like brothers, do we.

BEN: No. I guess not.

MICHAEL: Let me see your hands.

(BEN *and* MICHAEL *hold out their hands beside each other.*)

MICHAEL: Let me see your feet.

(BEN *and* MICHAEL *both unfold their legs and put their feet side by side.*)

BEN: I wonder who we look like.

Scene 13

(LORNA's apartment)

(LORNA's asleep on the couch. BERT is gone.)

MAGGIE: *(O S)* Lorna? Hey, Lorna? *(She bangs on the door.)* Lorna! Open up!

(LORNA finally comes to. Stumbles to the door)

LORNA: What?

MAGGIE: *(O S)* Open up!

(LORNA opens the door. MAGGIE stands holding the arm of CELIA, nineteen, who's trying to wrestle her way out of MAGGIE's grip. She wears an old back pack and looks as if she's been on the road for too many of those nineteen years.)

MAGGIE: She says she's yours.

CELIA: I didn't say anything.

MAGGIE: You did too. You said your mother lived in the building.

CELIA: How do you know it's her?

MAGGIE: Look at you.

CELIA: So?

MAGGIE: Look at her.

(CELIA looks LORNA over. LORNA is disheveled.)

CELIA: I look like that?

MAGGIE: There's certainly something familiar there.

CELIA: I think I'm much prettier.

MAGGIE: You do, do you? *(She compares the two.)* Well, yes, well, maybe you're right.

(LORNA closes the door.)

LORNA: No one looks like familiar here! *(She listens, panicked, by the door. She waits, then opens the door.)*

(CELIA *stands alone on the other side.*)

(LORNA *doesn't close the door. Remains staring*)

CELIA: Take a picture. It lasts longer.

MAGGIE: Oh my.

LORNA: Take a hike Maggie.

(LORNA *moves away from the door,* CELIA *walks inside.*)

(CELIA *looks the apartment over as* LORNA *looks her over.* CELIA *sets down her back pack.*)

LORNA: You're not staying here—

CELIA: I didn't say I was.

LORNA: Keep it on.

(CELIA *puts it on her back.*)

CELIA: Bitch.

LORNA: What?

CELIA: Nothing.

(LORNA *tries to clean herself up. Adjust her hair. Her dress*)

LORNA: What do you want?

(CELIA *sees her heels by the couch.*)

CELIA: Nice. (*She slips off her clogs and puts them on.*) Same size. How do I look?

LORNA: Take them off.

CELIA: Why?

LORNA: Your feet are dirty.

(CELIA *slips them off.*)

CELIA: Well then. Can I use your shower?

LORNA: No.

CELIA: I could use a shower.

LORNA: You're not staying here.

CELIA: Did I say I was? *(She picks up objects around the room.)*

LORNA: Look—

CELIA: Celia.

LORNA: Celia—

CELIA: Do you like it?

LORNA: What?

CELIA: My name?

LORNA: I don't know—

CELIA: They said they told you what it would be.

LORNA: Who?

CELIA: My parents. When they gave you the check, they said they told you my name.

LORNA: I don't remember.

CELIA: Celia E Brown. The E doesn't stand for anything. Did they tell you that?

LORNA: I don't know—

CELIA: My parents just liked the letter. Do you like it?

LORNA: What?

CELIA: E?

(LORNA stares at her.)

CELIA: I tell people it was taken from the eye doctor's chart. So I could always be seen.

(LORNA looks away.)

CELIA: Mother.

LORNA: Don't call me that.

CELIA: What?

LORNA: Don't call me that.

CELIA: But—

LORNA: Please.

CELIA: It's true. I'm here. Look at me.

LORNA: I know.

CELIA: Look at me—

LORNA: I know. Isn't that enough?

(CELIA *sets down her guitar and back pack and sits beside* LORNA *on the couch.*)

LORNA: What do you want?

CELIA: I want you to look at me.

LORNA: Why?

CELIA: Please.

LORNA: Why?

CELIA: I need you to tell me things.

LORNA: I see you.

CELIA: Look at me.

LORNA: I said, I see you!

CELIA: Do you?

LORNA: Yes.

CELIA: Do you?

LORNA: Leave me alone. I lead a quiet life—

(CELIA *presents her body to* LORNA.)

CELIA: Do you see my, my fingers?

LORNA: I don't bother people—

CELIA: Look at them. They were tiny when you saw them last time, weren't they? Grabbing things? They're big now. Strong. They're the same fingers. Grabbing—

LORNA: I mind my own business—

CELIA: See my hair. It comes from you. Tangled. My lips. Hungry and cold. My eyes.

(LORNA *keeps her eyes covered.*)

CELIA: Scared and vacant. My lashes. They grew from you. Dark. Long. Flirtatious—

LORNA: Please—

CELIA: My belly.

LORNA: No—

CELIA: My feet. Look at them.

LORNA: No.

CELIA: See my feet. They want to run like yours.

LORNA: I don't care.

CELIA: They want to run away all the time.

LORNA: Please—

CELIA: Tell me why they want to run.

LORNA: Don't do this.

CELIA: Tell me why.

LORNA: Please leave—

CELIA: Tell me why they ache at night. Your blood pumping through them—

LORNA: No.

CELIA: Mother—

LORNA: Please, girl. Stop.

CELIA: Tell me why they look like yours.

LORNA: I'm not going to tell you I'm sorry—

CELIA: Tell me why they look like yours and it doesn't matter.

LORNA: I'm not going to apologize.

CELIA: Tell me why my feet cry at night when they are alone. Why they sleep with others they don't even know.

LORNA: I'm not going to lie.

CELIA: Tell me why I am your daughter and I don't even know you.

LORNA: I won't make excuses.

CELIA: Tell me why I am your daughter and you don't love me.

LORNA: I don't know who you are.

CELIA: Tell me why I want to rip your heart out and throw it away.

(LORNA *finally looks at* CELIA.)

LORNA: I am not sorry.

CELIA: Tell me why I want to crawl back inside you.

LORNA: I did nothing wrong.

CELIA: Tell me how you sold me.

LORNA: I had to live.

END OF ACT ONE

ACT TWO

Scene 14

(The street)

(BEN and MICHAEL stumble drunk arm in arm across the stage.)

MICHAEL: That's right.

BEN: How many times?

MICHAEL: Oh, that's not important.

BEN: Did they try and find you?

MICHAEL: Oh, no, I always went home. Eventually.

BEN: Why?

MICHAEL: I don't like the cold much.

BEN: No.

MICHAEL: Or hunger.

BEN: No.

MICHAEL: A bed is nice too.

BEN: I would never run away.

MICHAEL: You would if there was a fist coming at you.

BEN: Maybe.

MICHAEL: Let me tell you something, Benjamin, from one brother to another— You ever read *Frankenstein*?

BEN: No.

MICHAEL: If there's one thing I know about, it's people. I've got eyes like a hawk for watching people, and I think that if anyone were to come ten feet within your soft soul with an object meant to harm your, you—how tall are you?

BEN: Why?

MICHAEL: Don't worry. Look at me. You can always be a late bloomer—

(BEN *lets go of* MICHAEL.)

BEN: Maybe, maybe my dad was short.

MICHAEL: He could be a dynamo.

BEN: Sure.

MICHAEL: If Lorna wanted him, hell. Right?

BEN: I'll ask her.

MICHAEL: You do that.

BEN: What are you going to ask her?

MICHAEL: Oh, well, you know. The usual.

BEN: Usual what?

MICHAEL: Usual son to mother questions concerning birth control and did she ever consider using it.

BEN: Oh.

MICHAEL: You think that's too much?

BEN: No. But, what do you think she's going to tell you?

MICHAEL: Some romance story.

BEN: Then why ask her?

MICHAEL: I'm a hopeless romantic.

BEN: Hey. Me too.

Scene 15

(LORNA's *apartment*)

(LORNA *enters from the bedroom and finds* CELIA *sleeps curled up on the couch.*)

(LORNA *approaches* CELIA. *She touches a piece of* CELIA's *hair. Smells it*)

(LORNA *grabs a blanket and begins to put it on* CELIA, *but in doing so, hesitates. She throws the blanket on a chair.*)

(LORNA *lights a cigarette. Grabs her keys, and exits.*)

(CELIA *wakes.*)

Scene 16

(*The hall. A line of doors. A baby cries off stage.*)

(LORNA *rushes forward and falls into a drunk* MICHAEL *and* BEN.)

(*There's little space to pass.*)

LORNA: Where are you going?

BEN: Home—

MICHAEL: Where are you going?

LORNA: You get him drunk too?

MICHAEL: You going to ground us?

LORNA: Let me through.

MICHAEL: Please ground us. Make us stay home.

LORNA: Let me through.

MICHAEL: Let Doctor Frankenstein through!

BEN: I think I'm going to be sick.

MICHAEL: "Oh! My creator, make me feel happy; let me feel gratitude towards you for one benefit! Let me see that I excite the sympathy of some existing thing; do not deny me my request!..."

MAGGIE: *(O S)* What's that noise?

BEN: I feel sick.

MAGGIE: *(O S)* Lorna?

BEN: I mean it—

LORNA: Not here—

MICHAEL: That's my boy.

BEN: Oh God— *(He starts to heave.)*

MAGGIE: *(O S)* Who's out there? I can call the cops, you know?

LORNA: Mother fucker.

(LORNA grabs BEN's arm and unlocks her apartment door.)

Scene 17

(The sound of BEN vomiting O S)

(LORNA's apartment)

(MICHAEL stands trying to light a cigarette.)

(LORNA enters pulling CELIA out of her bedroom.)

CELIA: I wasn't going to steal anything.

LORNA: Keep your hands off my stuff.

CELIA: I was just looking at it.

(CELIA sees MICHAEL before he focuses on her.)

CELIA: There's no crime against looking.

LORNA: Depends what you're looking for.

CELIA: You're a little young for her, aren't you?

MICHAEL: You jealous?

CELIA: Not yet.

MICHAEL: Don't worry then, Sunshine.

LORNA: None of this sunshine talk in here, kids. I'm not running a day care center. Get moving.

MICHAEL: What's your rush?

LORNA: I'm not here for your entertainment.

MICHAEL: You see me clapping?

LORNA: I don't know how you got my name and address, but I want it back. You hear? You're not taking any of it with you.

CELIA: I was just looking.

LORNA: A woman's got a right to her privacy.

MICHAEL: A kid has a right to meet his mother.

CELIA: His mother?

MICHAEL: Yeah.

CELIA: You're his mother?

LORNA: It's yet to be confirmed.

(BEN *enters from the bathroom wiping his mouth and pale.*)

BEN: Can, can I lay down?

LORNA: Jesus! Does this place look like a shoe?

MICHAEL: If the old woman has some kids—

LORNA: I am not old.

CELIA: He's yours too?

LORNA: So he says.

CELIA: Damn.

LORNA: So you all say.

CELIA: I have proof—

(LORNA *pours herself a drink.*)

LORNA: Listen, you three, I didn't ask for you here, did I? Did I? Did I send out invitations? Did I send out notices to come spend your goddamn summer vacation scratching around my door, looking for love?

MICHAEL: I am not looking for love—

CELIA: That's not why—

LORNA: Bullshit. That's what you all want.

CELIA: How much did you sell them for?

MICHAEL: What?

CELIA: She got twenty thousand dollars for me.

MICHAEL: No shit?

CELIA: Under the table.

MICHAEL: See, now that's interesting to me because all these years I just assumed I was left at the wrong door step.

CELIA: I'm sure she got some money for you.

LORNA: You're not sure of anything.

(CELIA *holds up a contract.*)

CELIA: I am sure that I am standing in my mother's apartment. I am sure that my mother sold me for twenty thousand dollars on August 9, 1979. I am sure that my father is unknown. I am sure that you were told my name before I was removed from the delivery room and placed in my parents' arms. I am sure that no contact was made with me after that day. I am sure no cards or presents were ever sent for my birthday. Or Christmas or any other holiday for that matter. And, I am sure that my child will never see a two-page bill of sale—

LORNA: That is not what that—

CELIA: An *agreement* never to come claim her, with my name and signature and *price* on her head.

LORNA: Don't be so sure until you've been there.

CELIA: I am there.

(LORNA *is silent.*)

MICHAEL: A price. Now that's an interesting subject. How much did you get for me?

LORNA: I would like you all to leave now.

MICHAEL: See, that never even occurred to me, Mom, because I just assumed I was some orphan my parents took pity on in a sea of tiny beds, and they thought they could do with me what they will. A shitty home is better than none…but now, see…now it makes sense that really they didn't get what they paid for, and I know how they hate that, and that must have been terribly disappointing. Not to mention, a bad investment.

LORNA: It wasn't that simple.

MICHAEL: Oh, but I think it was Mom.

LORNA: Don't call me that.

MICHAEL: But Ma, the thing I want to know is…what I want to know is what gave you the right to bring a new child into the world, with his bloody skin and bare butt in the air and his eyes closed shut and his mouth still wailing to heaven as they cut the cord—who gave you the right to bring him forth and then decide he'd be better off in the arms of strangers?

LORNA: I gave me the right.

MICHAEL: I see. And is that a halo I see around your hair or just a bad case of bed head?

LORNA: You're here, aren't you?

MICHAEL: Yes. This is true. I am here. But your head, this room, my head and the four of us combined, are not big enough to hold all the horrors and loneliness I endured with those strangers and if you for one moment think you are some angel of mercy, I think you better have yourself another drink because I am here to tell you, you are WRONG.

LORNA: They wanted a baby.

MICHAEL: You think every couple that can't have a baby together deserves one?

CELIA: If they have the money?

MICHAEL: Right. Yes. If they have the money?

LORNA: I think they should have the chance to have one, yes. I gave them that.

BEN: I like my parents—

MICHAEL: You are not God—

LORNA: No, but I gave them something beautiful—

MICHAEL: You sold some babies because you could, but you have no right to claim that what you did was always in the best interest of the child. No. No right. I am here to tell you that you were WRONG.

LORNA: How could I know that?

MICHAEL: You couldn't. I guess you couldn't. But the least you could do is take some responsibil—

LORNA: What do you want me to do? Hug you?

(MICHAEL *bats the drink out of* LORNA's *hands.*)

MICHAEL: Look me in the eye! That's what I want you to do! Look me in the fucking eye!

(LORNA *looks at* MICHAEL.)

MICHAEL: "How dare you sport thus with life!"

LORNA: What?

MICHAEL: I am your son! You made me!

LORNA: You want me to kiss you?

MICHAEL: I want more!

LORNA: More what?

MICHAEL: I want to be happy.

LORNA: Me too.

MICHAEL: Why did you have me? *(Silence)* For profit? *(Silence)*

LORNA: Go figure it out. *(She opens the door.)* Go out there and figure it out. Make yourselves proud. All of you. Go walk the earth. Jump the moon. Crawl into someone arms. But not mine.

CELIA: Are there more?

LORNA: Why? You want to call them up? Bring them over? Peck me to death?

BEN: We wouldn't do that.

CELIA: Are there more?

LORNA: What's it matter?

MICHAEL: See again, what interests me about you, Madre, is that you still seem to lack certain obvious emotions or regard or Responsibility concerning your children—

LORNA: Listen—

MICHAEL: We continue to ask you questions about you, your past, our lineage, and you still seem unaware that it is of great importance to us.

LORNA: And you seem to lack the obvious awareness that I don't care. No matter how many *Frankenstein* quotes you throw at me. You are not a monster.

MICHAEL: How do you know?

(LORNA notices something wet on her shirt. Across her chest)

LORNA: It's not in your blood.

MICHAEL: I'm not so sure… But, still, you didn't see how I was raised now did you?

(LORNA *hides the spot with her arm.*)

CELIA: How many others are there, Lorna?

LORNA: You found me. You can find them.

BEN: I just want to find my father.

LORNA: If you do, tell him I said hi.

BEN: O K—

MICHAEL: There's not one single thing, not one bit of yourself you'd like to impart upon us, your dear children? Your own flesh and blood? From your very own womb?

(LORNA *thinks.*)

LORNA: Maybe one thing.

(*All three stand looking at her. Waiting*)

LORNA: I don't love you. (*She holds the door.*) I never did.

(*Slowly they file out.*)

(LORNA *closes the door behind them and checks her shirt. It's wet through. Milk has started to pour from her breasts.*)

LORNA: No… Oh no you don't.

MAGGIE: (*O S*) What's all the commotion down here?

LORNA: No. I won't have it.

(LORNA *takes off her shirt. Her bra is soaked with milk.*)

MAGGIE: (*O S*) Hey Lorna? What's going on in there?

LORNA: Nothing! (*She covers herself. She's panicked.*)

MAGGIE: (*O S*) Who were all those kids? Your kids?

LORNA: I don't have time for you, Maggie. (She puts the blanket up to her chest. She picks up the phone. Bert…come get me…I'm just asking you to…because I need you to come get me…I am being invaded again…

MAGGIE: (*O S*) Lorna!

LORNA: *(In phone)* I'm being swarmed, Bert.

Scene 18

(The beach)

*(*CELIA, MICHAEL *sit staring at the water.)*

MICHAEL: Guess there won't be cake.

CELIA: Or balloons.

MICHAEL: Who's the father?

CELIA: Of?

MICHAEL: The one in your belly.

CELIA: Oh. Would you know him?

MICHAEL: Lucky guy.

CELIA: Thanks.

MICHAEL: Too bad incest is so unpopular.

CELIA: Right.

MICHAEL: I could have made a move on you.

CELIA: I wouldn't have stopped you.

MICHAEL: See?

CELIA: We've got trouble in our genes.

MICHAEL: Lust in our loins.

CELIA: Hunger in our hearts.

MICHAEL: Adultery in our underpants.

CELIA: Sorry.

MICHAEL: I'm a crappy boyfriend anyway.

CELIA: I'm unfaithful.

MICHAEL: I cry.

CELIA: I'm jealous.

MICHAEL: I don't mix well at parties.

CELIA: I make scenes.

MICHAEL: I drink too much.

CELIA: I'm pregnant.

MICHAEL: I'm moody.

CELIA: It could have been wonderful.

MICHAEL: Paradise.

(BEN *enters with a stack of papers.*)

BEN: I want to go home.

MICHAEL: Why?

BEN: Look at this.

MICHAEL: How many?

BEN: Twelve.

CELIA: No. (*She grabs the papers.*)

BEN: I've never felt so lonely in all my life.

MICHAEL: You're young. Have faith.

BEN: I feel miserable.

MICHAEL: They'll be plenty more of that.

BEN: I want my mother.

(MICHAEL *looks over* CELIA's *shoulder. They read the paper together.*)

CELIA: "Michael, July 8th, 1974 Columbus, Ohio"

MICHAEL: "Ben, June 20, 1976, Louisville, Kentucky"

BEN: "Celia, August 9, 1979, Bedford, New Hampshire"

CELIA & MICHAEL: "Alice, December 4, 1982, Norfolk, Virginia"

(BEN *joins in.*)

BEN, CELIA & MICHAEL: "Kate, December 15, 1984, Virginia Beach, Virginia"…

Scene 19

(LORNA's apartment)

LORNA: And then there was Kate and she wasn't born right and they put her away…she wasn't what any of us expected so we just had to put her away. So I, well I…

BEN, CELIA & MICHAEL: (O S) "Emma, May 3, 1987, Raleigh, North Carolina"

LORNA: But Emma. She was fine. I just was so happy she was fine.

BEN, CELIA & MICHAEL: (O S) "Pete, April 7, 1989, Atlanta, Georgia"

LORNA: I got a lot of money for Pete.

BERT: Why?

LORNA: They really wanted a boy.

BEN, CELIA & MICHAEL: (O S) "Paul, September 23, 1991, Phoenix, Arizona"

LORNA: Paul didn't cry for hours. They almost wanted their money back. But then he wailed. I could hear him across the hall and them trying to quiet him.

BEN, CELIA & MICHAEL: (O S) "Star, October 12, 1993, Santa Fe, New Mexico"

LORNA: They wanted to call her Star and I couldn't say anything. She looked nothing like a Star…she was more plain. Grounded. More of a Sam really…

BEN, CELIA & MICHAEL: (O S) "Bette, October 11, 1995, Flagstaff, Arizona"

LORNA: Her parents were older and they had a friend named Bette and they thought she looked just like her. Her hands were tight fists I remember. A boxer. She punched the air.

BEN, CELIA & MICHAEL: *(O S)* "Jack, February 7, 1997, Eugene, Oregon"

LORNA: It was a difficult birth. I was in labor for thirty hours. It had always been so easy, and then when Jack finally came, I fell asleep before I got to see him… and…

BEN, CELIA & MICHAEL: *(O S)* "Lily, July 1, 1999, Portland, Oregon."'

LORNA: Her skin was like a hazelnut. She was very quiet. Sweet. Round. Smiling. *(She passes a glance to* BERT.*)* I like the name Lily. It was my mother's name. *(She touches her breasts and they are still soaked through with milk.)* I didn't mean to hurt them, Bert.

BERT: I know.

LORNA: A woman has to live. People want babies.

BERT: Yeah.

LORNA: Some people will do whatever they have to to get them. Really.

BERT: Sure.

LORNA: I can have them. It's easy for me.

BERT: Sure.

LORNA: It's not so easy for everyone.

BERT: I know.

LORNA: A woman's got to live. Support herself. I don't have other skills.

BERT: Well—

LORNA: I didn't go to college. I didn't even finish high school. I could pick cotton. That's it.

BERT: Huh.

LORNA: Shit. This is what I could do and they're here.

(BERT *is silent.*)

LORNA: Right?

BERT: Right.

LORNA: Answer me.

BERT: I did.

LORNA: What difference does it make how they got here? ...Bert?

BERT: What?

LORNA: What difference does it make?

BERT: What's your mother's name again?

LORNA: Lily.

BERT: Are you sure?

LORNA: Of course I'm sure.

BERT: Positive?

LORNA: Yes!

BERT: Why are you getting angry with me?

LORNA: I think I know my own mother's name.

BERT: You do?

LORNA: Yes!

BERT: Sure now?

LORNA: Yes!

BERT: What difference does it make?

LORNA: Fuck you.

BERT: She's just some lady—

LORNA: I went to visit Kate—I, I visit her when I can.
I send her clothes and the doctors told me it wasn't
something I did wrong. They promised me. I made
sure of that—

BERT: Some woman—

LORNA: Michael's parents made it easy. They looked
so, so…Norman Rockwell; scrubbed and white-fenced
and she was mild and matronly and he grinned and
sold insurance and they had already bought the station
wagon outside—

BERT: She was just your mother—

LORNA: And then, then eventually, the more I had, and
the more exotic I made the kids, the more glamorous
that baby looked in wealthy arms, and the more money
they'd pay just to have it for themselves…and the
people found me…begging for babies…the couples
just found me and would pay anything for a newborn.
Anything—

BERT: Lily, you said her name was?

LORNA: Desperate for a newborn of their very own.

BERT: She wasn't important to you—

LORNA: Those kids have a mother.

BERT: They have two.

LORNA: I'm not the one that needs them!

BERT: What do you need?

LORNA: To enjoy my life.

BERT: That's it?

LORNA: *My* life. That's not much to ask.

BERT: They're not trying to take it away from you.

LORNA: Yes they are. They are. They want pieces of
it. They want reasons and stories and names and

pictures and faces and skin colors and eye colors
and freckles and birth marks and memories and
explanations I didn't save for them. I didn't even keep
them for myself. That's not what I do. I don't hold
on to things like that, I just run through them. I like
it that way. I like the way I do things and the money
all those couples gave me let me do it. It's not that
complicated. They wanted something they couldn't
make themselves, and I gave it to them. Like, like a
shoe smith. I gave them the right fit...but now all these
goddamn shoes are walking back here asking me what
type of leather I used and why didn't I wear them
myself and which goddamn cow forked over the skin.
I want my privacy back. I want my body back. They
look at it and they steal something from me and then
something starts to hurt. I feel this pull in my stomach
and my tits, look at my tits...but my mind...my mind
feels the same way I did when I turned over in that
delivery room with every one of them...it feels fifteen
miles down the road with a cigarette in my hand and
two year's rent in my pocket and they aren't getting
near it. They can take my tits with them, suck away...I
won't be using them...but they are not getting the
goods, you see...they're not getting the girl with it...
this is what keeps Lorna Cotes alive and free and they
aren't getting it.

BERT: Fine.

LORNA: I didn't mean to hurt them.

BERT: I know.

LORNA: I didn't.

BERT: I heard you.

LORNA: Take me to the hospital, Bert.

BERT: Why?

LORNA: Something's ripping me apart.

Scene 20

(The street. A motel sign flashes in the background.)

(BEN, CELIA and MICHAEL stand with suitcases and backpacks beside them.)

MICHAEL: We could start a band instead.

BEN: Or a basketball team.

CELIA: Our own cult.

MICHAEL: A traveling circus...trapeze artists...The Lost Lorna Twelve.

BEN: I hate traveling.

CELIA: Clowns scare me.

BEN: I'm allergic to peanuts.

MICHAEL: I'm...well. Heights are not my...

(BEN checks his watch.)

BEN: I told my parents I'd be home on the next plane.

MICHAEL: Don't be a stranger.

BEN: I won't.

CELIA: Call us when you get home.

BEN: I will.

MICHAEL: And don't forget to brush your teeth and say your prayers.

BEN: I won't. *(He picks up his suitcase. It's heavy in his arms.)*

MICHAEL: Hey, you know what I think?

BEN: What?

MICHAEL: I think your dad must be someone huge.

BEN: You think?

MICHAEL: Oh yeah. I think he's probably a king somewhere or something.

BEN: No…

CELIA: I think Michael's right. I see royalty in you.

BEN: You do?

MICHAEL: Something we don't have.

BEN: Really?

CELIA: We're, we're just common chicken stock.

MICHAEL: Run of the mill.

BEN: What is it?

CELIA: Is it his hair, Michael?

MICHAEL: Well, that's certainly nice, but I think it's more than that.

CELIA: Right…right…something in his face?

MICHAEL: It's certainly a noble face, great nose—

CELIA: Oh yes. And eyes.

MICHAEL: Strong.

CELIA: Definitely.

(BEN *touches his nose.*)

MICHAEL: But you know, I think it's in his shoulders. His shoulders have a stance all their own.

(BEN *takes a look at himself.*)

CELIA: They are going places.

MICHAEL: Indeed. They are. I think your father must be a great man, Benjamin. You are the product of some excellent genes.

CELIA: Grade A.

MICHAEL: It's written all over you.

BEN: Really?

CELIA: In gold.

MICHAEL: It surrounds you.

BEN: Wow. You know what's funny?

MICHAEL: What?

BEN: My parents are always telling me to stand up straight. Keep my head up. Always.

MICHAEL: Are they?

BEN: "Such a great mind and big heart is wasted on a guy who can't hold it up high."

MICHAEL: They sound like smart people.

BEN: I thought they were just nagging me.

CELIA: They're lucky to have you.

MICHAEL: Don't let them forget it.

(They stand in silence.)

MICHAEL: Take care of yourself. Keeps your nose clean.

BEN: You too.

MICHAEL: Are you trying to tell me what to do, little brother?

BEN: No.

MICHAEL: I don't want to have to kick your ass.

(BEN *turns to* CELIA.)

BEN: Good, good luck with your baby.

CELIA: Thanks.

BEN: He's the lucky kid.

CELIA: You think so, huh?

BEN: He's got one, two…five uncles. Six aunts.

CELIA: Right.

(BEN *picks up his suitcase.)*

BEN: I'm going to tell my mom about you guys. She won't believe it.

MICHAEL: You don't have to tell her about the drunk part.

BEN: Are you kidding? (*He smiles as he walks off stage.*)

(MICHAEL *reaches and pulls* CELIA *to him and kisses her.*)

MICHAEL: The forbidden fruit is always sweeter. Isn't it.

CELIA: Where'd you learn to kiss?

MICHAEL: What do you mean?

CELIA: You nearly took my teeth out.

MICHAEL: I did not.

CELIA: You did. You can't get a girl like that.

MICHAEL: I've gotten lots of girls like that.

CELIA: Uh huh.

MICHAEL: They throw themselves at me—

(CELIA *grabs* MICHAEL *and kisses him. He doesn't want to let go.*)

CELIA: Now that is a kiss.

MICHAEL: Uh huh.

CELIA: Remember it.

MICHAEL: I'll try.

CELIA: And don't waste it on just anybody.

MICHAEL: Huh?

CELIA: They'll think you're easy.

MICHAEL: Uh huh.

CELIA: Believe me.

MICHAEL: Sure.

CELIA: Michael?

MICHAEL: Yeah?

CELIA: Do me a favor?

MICHAEL: What?

(MICHAEL *moves in to kiss* CELIA *again.*)

CELIA: Tell me it's all going to work out.

MICHAEL: What?

CELIA: Just tell me I can be a good mother.

MICHAEL: You can.

CELIA: How do you know?

MICHAEL: Well…you like babies, right?

CELIA: Yes.

MICHAEL: See. There's a start.

CELIA: I guess. Fuck. (*She begins to cry.*) Fuck.

MICHAEL: C'mon, Celia.

CELIA: I'm gonna fuck up.

MICHAEL: No. You won't.

CELIA: I will. I fuck things up. All the time.

MICHAEL: You won't this. (*Silence*) Hold out your arms.

CELIA: What?

MICHAEL: Hold out your arms.

(CELIA *holds out her arms.*)

MICHAEL: Nice, long arms. Wow. Strong?

(CELIA *makes a muscle.*)

MICHAEL: Yes. Very strong. Good. Now do this.

(MICHAEL *makes a cradle with his arms.* CELIA *copies him.*)

MICHAEL: O K. Now sway your arms back and forth.

(CELIA *sways her arms, as if a baby is inside.*)

MICHAEL: Uh huh. Great. Now whisper in your baby's ear. Softly. "I love you".

CELIA: "I love you."

MICHAEL: Softer than that.

CELIA: "I love you."

MICHAEL: "I always will."

CELIA: "I always will."

MICHAEL: "You're the most perfect child there is."

CELIA: "You're the most perfect child there is."

MICHAEL: "I'll never leave you."

CELIA: "I'll never leave you."

MICHAEL: "I'll never hurt you."

CELIA: "I'll never hurt you."

MICHAEL: "I'm your mother."

CELIA: "I'm your mother."

MICHAEL: "Aren't we lucky?"

CELIA: "Aren't we lucky?"

MICHAEL: "You're home."

CELIA: "You're always home."

Scene 21

(Hospital room)

(LORNA lies in bed sleeping. BERT sits in a chair beside her.)

(MAGGIE enters with a rather wilted flowering plant.)

MAGGIE: Since when did cabs start costing twenty bucks just to go one way?

BERT: Hey Maggie.

MAGGIE: One way!

BERT: Thanks for coming.

MAGGIE: Well, pretty much spent a month's worth of groceries just getting over here but I didn't want her to think I don't care about her or something. *(She sets the plant down. It loses a few leaves.)* Four dollars they wanted for this thing. How's she doing?

BERT: Alright. She's coming in and out of sleep—

MAGGIE: They take everything out?

BERT: No.

MAGGIE: Well, it would be easier if you ask me. Might as well just rip it all out and forget about it.

BERT: Maybe—

MAGGIE: She's no spring chicken and she sure as hell doesn't have any plans for a family, no, I know she's not that type, so why not just take it all out.

BERT: She might feel empty.

MAGGIE: Pssh. No. I had a complete hysterectomy twenty years ago and I felt fine. But of course, we didn't have much of a choice then.

(BERT is silent.)

MAGGIE: She'll be alright. She's a tough old bird. Nice hospital. Wonder how much a night they want for this room.

LORNA: *(Sleepy)* None of your business.

MAGGIE: Well, there she is.

LORNA: Hi Maggie.

MAGGIE: How're you feeling?

LORNA: I'd love a drink.

MAGGIE: You know it cost me twenty bucks for the ride down here?

LORNA: Really?

MAGGIE: It's ridiculous. You'd think I could ride in a limo or something with those prices.

LORNA: Thanks for coming.

MAGGIE: Oh, well, you know. You look good.

LORNA: Thanks.

MAGGIE: And you'll heal real fast.

(LORNA *nods.*)

MAGGIE: It's sure quiet at home now without you.

(MICHAEL *enters carrying a single flower.*)

MAGGIE: And no kids running around the halls.

LORNA: Uh huh.

MAGGIE: I'm still watching for you on T V.

LORNA: Thanks. Hey Bert, you want to give Maggie a ride home.

BERT: Oh. Yeah.

LORNA: I'd appreciate it.

BERT: Sure.

MAGGIE: I just got here.

LORNA: I don't want you to miss your shows.

MAGGIE: Oh, that's alright—

LORNA: Is it Saturday night?

MAGGIE: I guess I should get back. I really don't like the smell of this place anyway. Smells like some disease is gonna sneak in and grab me while I'm here.

LORNA: Uh huh.

MAGGIE: Makes me feel old.

LORNA: I know.

MAGGIE: Well then. (*She touches* LORNA's *hand and then awkwardly kisses* LORNA's *forehead.*) You feel better now.

LORNA: Thanks.

MAGGIE: I'll water your plants.

(LORNA *nods as they exit.*)

(MICHAEL *moves closer.*)

(LORNA *sneaks a cigarette from under her pillow and lights it. She takes a deep drag.*)

MICHAEL: That'll kill you.

(LORNA *keeps smoking.*)

LORNA: So will a lot of things.

MICHAEL: I guess so.

LORNA: But hell…what do I know, I've got enough drugs in me to fly a horse. (*Silence. She puts out the cigarette. Getting sleepy again*) A present, huh?

MICHAEL: I heard you were here.

LORNA: Nice.

(MICHAEL *tries to hand* LORNA *the flower as she is falling asleep. He begins to set in on her chest—*)

LORNA: You're no monster, Michael. (*She grabs his hand instead. She falls asleep.*)

(MICHAEL *remains holding* LORNA's *hand. He studies her hand in his.*)

MICHAEL: "A mother bird sat on her egg…" (*He brings her hand to his cheek.*)

(MICHAEL *recites the book* Are You My Mother? *by P D Eastman, word for word, by heart. He tells* LORNA *the story in her sleep. As he finishes the last line, "…And you are my mother". He lays his head on* LORNA's *lap.*)

(LORNA *opens her eyes. She is awake.*)

(*Black out*)

END OF PLAY

CPSIA information can be obtained
at www.ICGtesting.com
Printed in the USA
LVHW04s0915180518
577628LV00002B/29/P